Exhale The Ocean From Orbit

Alchemy øf Poetry

BookLeaf
Publishing

Presentation by *BookLeaf Publishing*

Web: www.bookleafpub.com

E-mail: info@bookleafpub.com

ISBN: 9789357619677

First edition 2022

PREFACE

This here is where it begins.
The fall down deep into the heart of love and
longing.

Float

(A cloud in decipher of what shape
to mold into before forming into nullity.)
I become floated in the idea
of what would've been between us.
(Bouncing off different scenarios of stars yet
exploding inside a series of nullities)
Only..
I have been drowning in the depths of hope that
we could still be.
(A planet falling from orbit, drifting off to frozen
abyss.)
I wander to lost Realm,
for my infinite
existence.

Beckon

Would you come fall,
into my tides.
Leave upon those shores
swimming through currents.
This ocean once beckoned still flows
in the colour you had desired in
flowing past.
(Blue
emptiness of space
only awaits to be drunk
in by your Purple ecstasy)
Guiding into my own.
If I may,
wash
away
clean
all these worries and
doubts
built upon your lands.
Towering high in the castles of stone.
Let me bereft your soil, of
blackened past.
To give thy nature, a blooming love
to engulf infinitely as your own.

Flooding Heaven

Undress me,
like receding oceans.
In tides,
wash away all of these flaws.
Let me come clean from buried sin
anchored deep within.
With waves,
flood into me your love.
Let drown, i
unto your heavens, so
we may reach for eternity
Unleash in currents,
you in all torrential.
Lead,
me gasping for oxygen
but with only a need to
breathe
you
in.

Cold Veins

Deepest.
(Atlantis)
Where veins gone blue,
(come)
flow,
(t'wards)
in discover of your
answer,
(this love)
to this frozen heart.
i at depth,
(hold close)
apologize
in drowning
(my aching)
oceans
(breath)
of deluging
(of your touch)
immensity.

Heartbeats

I can only watch my own breaking,
at the core of this existence.
Falling down the continuum,
endlessly grasping onto nothing.

(eternally, eternity)
I reach out with faith only in..
I reach out with faith only in
your hands.

Can't I fall,
melting
within your palms, my love.
Can't I fall,
inwards,
within your heart, my love.

(O' how I wish your hands
were within mine,
your head embraced 'gainst
my chest.
Our beatings of hearts echoing
together,
through the expanse.)

Fracture

Could.
Upon fractured sky,
and heart
Could you hold close
(hold closed)
The tears,
bleeding off shores in
flood.
With moon and pale skin
wounds
(in broken frame)
I fall neath,
reflection in blue's deep.
Withering to,
our love drowned.
This is where I breathe in
restless
(restless)
agony in smile
(smile)

Fragments, Seamed

Even in fragments.
i fall closer amidst the dust
scattered specs to ancient grain
Is this where I feel.
(Exhale)
A life to not call home
i hear that the sky is calling,
faint whispers of winds.
But is it telling, only
to breathe,
that i've lost my place
(Existence)
and need to leave
into another space
that could still never be
called
my own

Exhale Existence

Drown from me, these hauntings
crushing me; of existence.
(My one, only)
so that I may,
in finality;
breathe such beauty
of
our once love.
(Ever, after)

Merely Air

My lungs gasp your name,
I'm choking.
Suffocating deepened
blue,
bubbles of air sinking from existence
at the mere thought of
never seeing you
again.

Fill me
(an ocean)
Have me
(drowning)
Bring me
(without you)

Delicate Distance

Take forward a gaze into
your hands,
the softness, the delicate,
the whites of your lines,
the calm in your steady,
the innocence, fragile
Though do you not feel.
my soul slowly oozing out from
the blackness in your eyes
as you stare me into
only becoming the distance
at the ending
over the silence at the beginning
snowfall

Pacific

I try not to become the ocean,
so to not be drowning under
my thoughts

Deep in darkened blue
I fall beneath
the pacific
raging against tides
this reality
has been crushing me
into sand

Down t'wards the abyss
I cater to the caverns below
leave me as a shipwreck
in hopes I get some rest

Dig out from trenches
this is where I can
be found
left in sails wrapped like
bandages
covering what rotting
wood

I have
now become

*(Come won't you..
Come won't..*

*..you rescue
me from these depths
O' Love)*

Sinking Of The Sea

Shall so and to call her the sea, that i
would've swam down with driven
immensity.
The deepest these weathered bones
would carry me, then only swim even
deeper
within
to where her deepest crevices and
secrets have been
immersed.
Buried neath.

This is where we could build our Atlantis.
This is where I'll drown in the idea of our love.
Within, such
currents holding me close.
In the encompassment of…

These are my last breaths holding in
thoughts of you.
Let me sustain this dream
even a little moment longer
before it bubbles unto
the abyss.

Becoming..
Burying beneath ancient grains.

I could have it fall into you hands
(as mine unworthy)
this heart,
(merely)
a precious stone
sinking.

Sacred Sky

And so watching
as the coloured sky,
drizzles to the ground,
like a slow desaturation
of these
once sacred
dreams.
Awaiting the frost,
a tundra to come
begin;
me into
a fading snowfall.
Having become frigid,
this blood frozen,
in time.
As withering,
to the nothingness.
i am now,
in reach
this abyss of
dissociated current

Black Holes

I have started to become bleeding,
the pouring of black holes from within.
a shroud,
of blackness envelopes
me against an uncertainty;
this self decimating anxiety
ever-
consuming,
now hollow from which I can-
not be free
Release from thee;
revolving
stars and their
screams
such
scars and dreams
orbiting this planet, i
have begun
falling
into
a vacuum; this void

Starving From The Weight

I hold tight,
this feeling.
As though I've been starving for centuries.
For this,
merely a touch
of your love,
within the fodder that I have become.

The weight of this continues crushing
me
down,
like sand,
blown from
existence,
the slipping of hope through my fingers as each
grain cuts deep,
of these failed hands.

That they were unable to give,
a place to hold safely,
in safety.

Locked In Shades

Intramural.
I've become locked in between
the sun and moon looking
for You.
Somewhere betwixt the shades
Of black and grey

Would you not bring me into white?
Will you not shower me
in light?
Must i only be confined to the night?

Ignite me,
I've come too close to the sun
placed with the red
and been set aflame.
Is this to be my destiny

Engulf me,
I've altered t'wards the moon
swept within the blue
encompassed only to
be immersed for eternity.

Bury me,
I've fallen back to the earth
grounded into the soil
Here is now where my fate lies.

Orbit

Come to;
the vacuum in which i.
orbit in,
my vastness of dark.
The planet that you be.
Surround me, your
nature,
envelop in;
the nurturing
love.
Watch,
the guiding of stars leading,
their light
across cosmos;
betwixt such grand
empty space.

We fall together in
universe.

The Mirror's Expression

To look into this
(to be wished)
blank expression
of a hand,
looking back
(back amongst her)
a lost heart
the broken pieces
reflecting,
(stardust)
dripping into
nothingness;
a void in
the black hole,
a distant star clinging on
to a wish.

Frozen Angel

O' Siren,
Upon your flakes of frozen touch
falling a light frost 'gainst
flesh,
dripping from your heavens,
let spill love,
into me;
Angel

Unfolding Rest

(In dissociation)
The night unfolds,
(bury me)
as my eyes close.
Only then again to reopen
(within the currents)
in a daylight folded into tundra's
blackness.
In frozen dream,
(awaiting Her embers touch)
clinging on to the cold,
i lay restless.

Unconditional

O' Love
If you had said you never wanted to see me
again.
Surely waves would tower from such a
torrential.
That waters would rise to the heavens,
as becoming one,
complete.

Crushing down,
flooding into organs
receding me,
into a
sanctuary
sea.

This watery tomb
at the darkest
depth
of abyss,
(must i call this home)
Though how ever
deep i may be
this love for you,
is unconditional.

And it was never about me,
so if I must, i would let you be,
i will endlessly drown
at the
bottom of this
deep blue sea.

(Please,
don't follow my
now hollow corpse
sinking
just so you can see
what it's like to be
drowning at the bottom
of my darkest blue
sea)

www.ingramcontent.com/pod-product-compliance
Lightning Source LLC
LaVergne TN
LVHW010854200726

843508LV00012B/2896